Getting Even

Contents

Welcome to Navigator Max

Guided Reading

Navigator Max offers accessible texts which will help you unlock the potential of guided reading with children who attain below the expected level for their chronological age in reading. *Navigator Max* is targeted at pupils entering Key Stage 2 at around National Curriculum level 2C.

Thus, *Navigator Max* complements its 'sister' programme, *Navigator*, which caters for the average to higher-achieving groups. Together, the two series provide a bank of fiction, non-fiction, poetry and plays for the majority of your class – with the flexibility to be used alongside your existing guided reading resources.

Navigator Max

Navigator Max comprises short stories, plays and graphic novels. The interest level is matched to the chronological age of the reader, while the reading age is lower. The writing is lively and the layout engaging, providing texts which will motivate and entertain while extending children's reading competence.

Navigator Max texts are designed for use in guided reading lessons and will support children, term by term, gradually introducing more complex language features, in line with the renewed Framework requirements. Used in conjunction with the Teaching Guides, the texts will enable you to deliver the relevant framework objectives, making classroom management easy, while giving children the pleasure of reading complete stories at an appropriate reading level.

A New Generation of Teacher Support

There is one Teaching Guide per term. Each Teaching Guide offers six focused guided reading sessions – two for each story, play or graphic novel – saving hours of valuable preparation time.

Each session is directed at the target group, having a text objective as its main focus, supported by additional word, sentence and text level work as appropriate. The objectives selected focus on the key skills and strategies these pupils need in order to make progress.

The session plans include questions for the teacher and sample responses that children might offer. Each session begins with simple recall and comprehension questions and moves on to more challenging open questions, which encourage discussion of, for example, characterisation, theme and choice of language. Also included are examples of statements which the teacher can add to the discussion. Teachers are advised to select from the possible questions and prompts, in order to target the needs of the children. This will enable children to develop higher order reading skills, essential for SATs preparation.

Quality Stories

Navigator Max fiction contains well-crafted stories by respected children's authors, which will capture children's enthusiasm for reading and writing.

Complete Fiction Genre Coverage

It can be difficult to find texts that are suitable for use in guided reading, particularly for children whose attainment in reading is below average. A great deal of planning time is required to find texts that match genre and objective requirements and which are also the right length and able to offer the appropriate level of challenge.

Navigator Max provides comprehensive coverage of the renewed Framework range requirements and objectives in a format suitable for lower attaining children.

Models for Writing

The short stories will serve as exemplar texts for children's own writing. The Teaching Guides also draw on the essential link between reading and writing.

Navigator Max and Assessment

Valuable information can be accrued during guided reading about children's application of essential reading skills and strategies. The Teaching Guides include questioning prompts to track a child's level of understanding of the teaching objective of the lesson. There are also links to the QCA Assessment Focuses for Reading. This will ensure that you have a clear picture of each child's progress.

Primary Framework Teaching Objectives

This table shows the objectives, taken from the renewed Framework for literacy, covered by the guided reading sessions in this book. You will find abbreviated versions of these objectives on the Teaching Guide pages, and a chart showing the coverage of these objectives for all books in this level in the Programme Handbook.

Getting Even – Traditional stories

		Session 1 / 2	Session 3 / 4
The Magic Paintbrush by Rosalind Kerven	Renewed Framework objectives	**Focus on Narrative Viewpoint** **Y5 Strand 3: 3** Understand the process of decision making **Y5 Strand 7: 2** Infer writers' perspectives from what is written and from what is implied	**Focus on Imagery** **Y5 Strand 7: 1** Make notes on and use evidence from across a text to explain events or ideas **Y5 Strand 7: 5** Explore how writers use language for comic and dramatic effects **Writing** **Y5 Strand 9: 2** Experiment with different narrative forms and styles to write their own stories
Theseus and the Minotaur retold by William Bedford	Renewed Framework objectives	**Focus on Narrative Viewpoint** **Y5 Strand 6: 1** Spell words containing unstressed vowels **Y5 Strand 7: 2** Infer writers' perspectives from what is written and from what is implied	**Focus on Imagery** **Y5 Strand 7: 1** Make notes on and use evidence from across a text to explain events or ideas **Y5 Strand 7: 5** Explore how writers use language for comic and dramatic effects **Writing** **Y5 Strand 9: 2** Experiment with different narrative forms and styles to write their own stories
The Giant's Eye by Jane Langford	Renewed Framework objectives	**Focus on Features of Traditional Stories and Graphic Novels** **Y5 Strand 7: 3** Compare different types of narrative and information texts and identify how they are structured **Y5 Strand 8: 2** Compare the usefulness of techniques such as visualisation, prediction and empathy in exploring the meaning of texts	**Focus on Treatment of Different Characters** **Y5 Strand 7: 1** Make notes on and use evidence from across a text to explain events or ideas **Y5 Strand 7: 2** Infer writers' perspectives from what is written and from what is implied **Writing** **Y5 Strand 9: 2** Experiment with different narrative forms and styles to write their own stories

How to use the Navigator Max Teaching Guides

TThere are two guided reading sessions for each story. Shorter Brown-level texts can be read to the end in the first session, then reread in the second session with a different focus. The reading of longer texts may be split between the two sessions. Each session is structured as follows.

Text introduction

This section prepares the children for independent reading by introducing subject matter and text type, and usually includes discussion, prediction and whole-group reading and/or analysis of a short section of text. The teacher should share the session objectives and success criteria with the children.

Teaching strategies

Suggestions are made for demonstrating and practising a particular reading strategy in relation to a specific phrase from the text. Children should apply it during independent reading.

Year 3 is a transition year: some pupils may not have completed all of their phonic work. Children reading the Brown-level books may be at this stage. In line with recommendations for the simple view of reading, *Navigator Max* uses phonics as the main reading strategy for this level. As children progress, they can use a range of strategies to help them when they are unsure what a word says, including the following:

Phonic knowledge: sound out the phonemes in words and blend them together.
- **Prompt:** does the <u>word on the page</u> *sound* like the <u>word you said</u>?

Graphic knowledge: look carefully at the letters / letter strings and the shape of the whole word.
- **Prompt:** does the <u>word on the page</u> *look* like the <u>word you said</u>? Do you recognise it?

Grammatical knowledge: think about what kind of word would fit in that part of the sentence.
- **Prompt:** does the word <u>fit in</u>?

Knowledge of context: think about what would make sense in the sentence and the story.
- **Prompt:** does the word <u>make sense</u>?

In addition, children should be prompted to:
- Attempt unknown words while thinking what word would fit and make sense.
- Continually check that what they are reading makes sense, by rereading and reading on, and then self-correcting errors.

Read and discuss

The teacher listens as children read part of the text independently. It is important to prompt and praise each child, while monitoring their reading fluency and comprehension. Observation gives important pointers to the progress of individual children. They then come back together for a group discussion before finishing the text. This ensures that children are reading the text independently with comprehension.

In order to allow all children to read the text at their own pace, record one of the 'Read and discuss' questions on the board. Those who finish early can think about the question on their own or with another member of the group while the others finish.

Focus on

Children are encouraged to read deeply into the text, using specific reading strategies to investigate one or two pages of the text, focusing on a key objective (usually text level).

Respond and return

The children reflect on the text as a whole, consolidating strategies and teaching objectives.

Follow-up

Two photocopy masters (PCMs) are provided for each story. The first focuses on the reading objective, the second on writing. These activities can be done:
- as independent tasks
- with the support of a Teaching Assistant
- as homework tasks.

Introduces the book and prepares children for independent reading

Demonstration of reading strategies

Independent reading and group discussion allows the teacher to check comprehension

One text level objective as main focus with one word or sentence level objective for each session

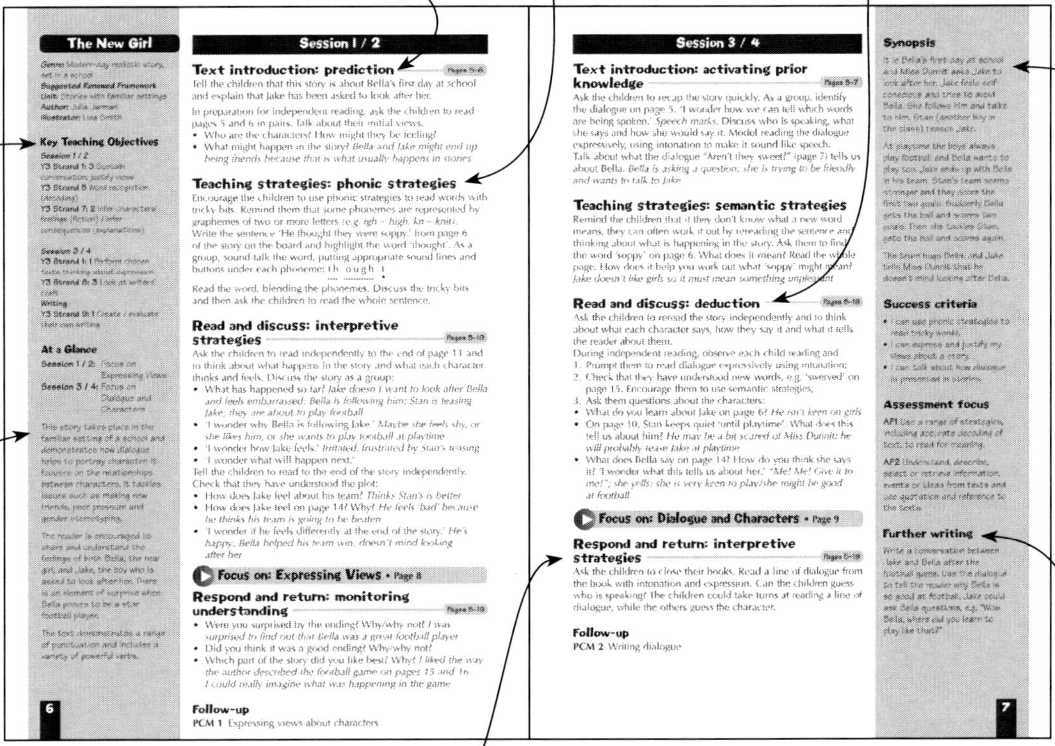

Overview of the literacy features of the text

Outline of the story

Returning to the text to explore specific teaching objectives

Link to writing, can be used as a follow-up task or as a guided writing session

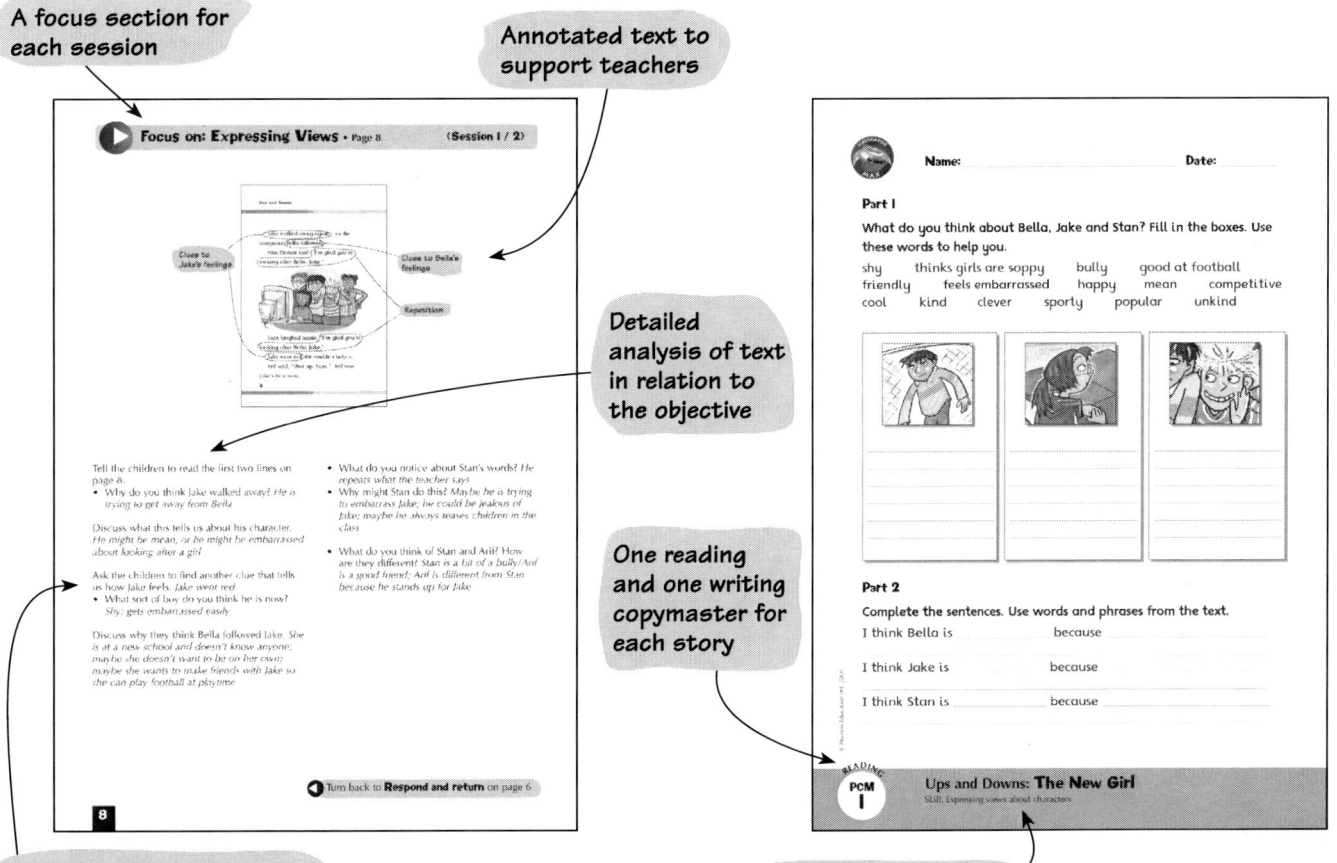

A focus section for each session

Annotated text to support teachers

Detailed analysis of text in relation to the objective

One reading and one writing copymaster for each story

Focused question prompts, from which the teacher selects to meet group needs

Clearly stated objective

Genre: Chinese folk tale
Suggested Renewed Framework
Unit: Traditional stories, fables, myths and legends
Author: Rosalind Kerven
Illustrator: Liz Pyle

Key Teaching Objectives

Session I / 2
Y5 Strand 3: 3 Understand process of decision making
Y5 Strand 7: 2 Infer writers' perspectives

Session 3 / 4
Y5 Strand 7: 1 Use evidence from a text to explain ideas
Y5 Strand 7: 5 Explore how writers produce comic / dramatic effects
Writing
Y5 Strand 9: 2 Write own story: experiment with different styles

At a Glance

Session I / 2:   Focus on
                 Narrative
                 Viewpoint
Session 3 / 4:   Focus on
                 Imagery

This story is set a long time ago in China. It is both mystical and magical, as the main character Ma Liang paints objects that then come alive.

The structure is that of a classic tale: a gift and challenge are given to the good character who has to overcome evil using his wits.

The tale includes figurative language, which creates vivid and powerful visual images.

Text introduction: activating prior knowledge
Page 5

Explain to the children that this is a traditional tale from China, set in ancient times. It is about a poor orphan boy called Ma Liang. Brainstorm features of folk tales: *mystical and magical; good triumphs over evil; a gift and challenge are given to the good character; strong moral messages; non-specific time.* Cover the picture on page 5 and read the introduction. Ask the children to work in pairs and to think of two key words to describe Ma Liang. Share their views of the character and the key words. Ask them to predict what may happen.

Teaching strategies: phonic/semantic strategies

Explain that a number of powerful descriptions give this story the feel of an ancient Chinese folk tale. Focus on pages 6 and 7. Read the sentence 'This brush was made by the gods from dragon pearls and stardust.' Discuss the meaning. Read it again, stopping at 'gods'. Talk about the effect of the additional information.
Write the words 'crouched', 'peach blossom' and 'outstretched'. Decode these words together using phonic strategies, then read each sentence. Check that the children understand what the words mean and remind them of semantic strategies for working out the meaning of unknown words.

Read and discuss: constructing images
Pages 5–9

Explain to the children that they will read half the story in this session. Ask them to read independently to the end of page 7 and to try to create pictures in their mind of each event. Discuss the story as a group:
- How does Ma Liang manage to do his art without any materials? *He makes everything he needs*
- What happens in Ma Liang's dream? *An old man gives him a paintbrush to help poor people*
- Read the last sentence on page 7. 'I wonder what this means. Is his head really spinning?'

Talk about what may happen next, then ask the children to read to the end of page 9. Check that they have understood the plot:
- What is on the floor when Ma Liang wakes? *The paintbrush*
- What happens when Ma Liang draws the horse? *It comes alive*
- Do you think the paintbrush is magic?

▶ Focus on: Narrative Viewpoint • Page 6

Respond and return: prediction
Pages 5–9

Ask the children what the old man told Ma Liang to do with the paintbrush. Discuss what they think Ma Liang will do next.
Look back at the list of features of traditional tales. Allocate one feature to each pair. Tell them to decide whether the feature is evident in the text and to find examples.

Follow-up
PCM 1 Investigating narrative viewpoint

Text introduction: monitoring understanding
Pages 5–9

Invite a member of the group to recap quickly what has happened so far. Discuss what makes the story sound like a traditional tale: *magical; challenge given to good character; non-specific time*
- What is missing from this traditional tale? *A bad character*
Ask the children to predict who the evil character might be and what they might do.

Teaching strategies: constructing images

Explain that the author has used imagery to help you see pictures in your head. Sentences using imagery do not always mean exactly what they say. For example, in 'his head spun with questions', his head was not really spinning. This expression helps us to understand how Ma Liang was feeling. When you read a sentence using imagery, you need to read the whole sentence and think about the picture it makes in your mind and what it could mean. Write on the board 'He painted more things in a fever of excitement.' and 'They sat down and ate until they almost burst.'. Read each sentence. Invite the children to share the pictures they have in their heads. Discuss what the sentences mean.

Read and discuss: interpretive strategies
Pages 10–18

Ask the children to read to the end of page 13. Discuss the story as a group:
- Explain how Ma Liang fulfils his promise. *He paints food for the poor*
- Who is the bad character? How do you know? *The wicked Emperor; clue in the name*
- Why does the Emperor demand gold? *Greedy; for himself*
- 'I wonder if Ma Liang will draw the mountain of gold.'
Tell the children to read to the end to find out if Ma Liang draws the mountain and whether the Emperor gets his gold. Check that the children have understood the plot:
- Why does Ma Liang feel angry? *Emperor is already very rich; lots of very poor subjects*
- How does Ma Liang trick the Emperor? *Puts treasure on an island and then creates a storm when the Emperor is sailing to the island*
- 'I wonder why Ma Liang went to a secret corner of China.' *So he would be left in peace to help the poor*

▶ Focus on: Imagery • Page 16

Respond and return: inference
Pages 5–18

Return to the list of features of traditional tales from Session 1 / 2. Does this story end like a traditional tale? Children can discuss:
- How the good character wins.
- The moral – does this story have a strong moral? What is it?

Follow-up

PCM 2 Writing an opening to a folk tale

Synopsis

Ma Liang is a poor orphan boy who longs to be an artist. One night he dreams that an old man gives him a paintbrush, made by the gods. The old man tells Ma Liang to promise only to only use the paintbrush to help the poor.

When Ma Liang wakes, he finds the paintbrush near his mat. He quickly learns that whatever he paints comes to life. True to his promise, he travels around helping the poor people of China.

An evil Emperor hears about the paintbrush and demands that Ma Liang paint him a mountain of gold. Ma Liang is angered by the Emperor's greed and draws a ship, which carries the Emperor out to sea. He is never seen again and Ma Liang is able to continue his good work.

Success criteria

- I can participate in group discussion and contribute to decision making.
- I can recognise and explain the narrative viewpoint.
- I can explain how the author uses imagery to create pictures for the reader.

Assessment focus

AF5 Explain and comment on writers' use of language, including grammatical and literary features at word and sentence level.

AF6 Identify and comment on writers' purposes and viewpoints and the overall effect of the text on the reader.

Further writing

Ask the children to imagine they are given a magic paintbrush. Tell them to draw four things they would paint and to describe each object, and how it could help people.

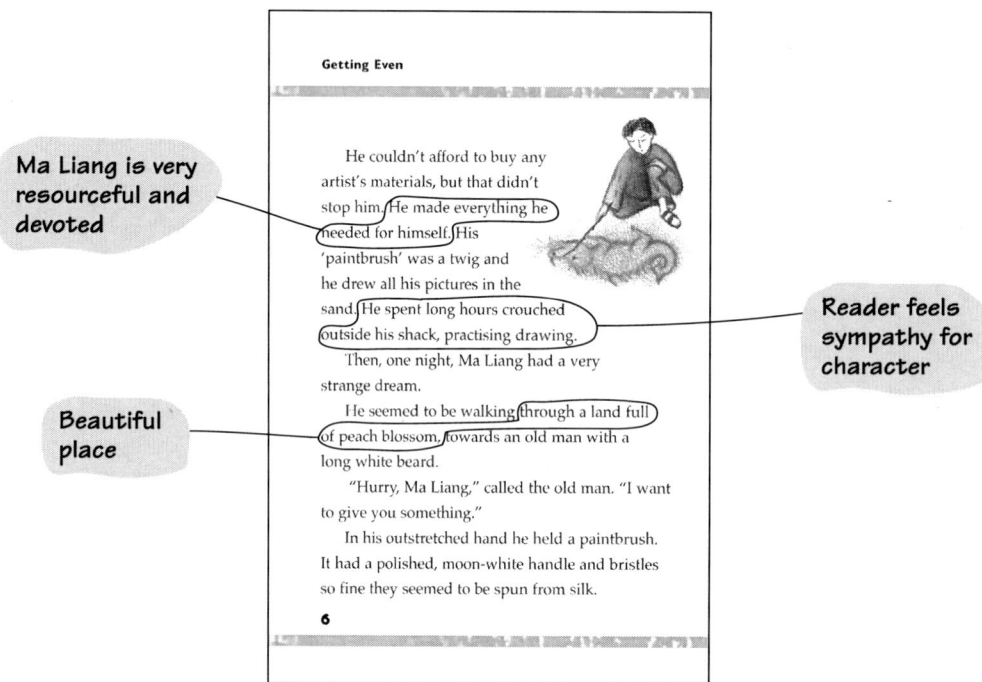

Ma Liang is very resourceful and devoted

Reader feels sympathy for character

Beautiful place

Getting Even

He couldn't afford to buy any artist's materials, but that didn't stop him. He made everything he needed for himself. His 'paintbrush' was a twig and he drew all his pictures in the sand. He spent long hours crouched outside his shack, practising drawing.

Then, one night, Ma Liang had a very strange dream.

He seemed to be walking through a land full of peach blossom, towards an old man with a long white beard.

"Hurry, Ma Liang," called the old man. "I want to give you something."

In his outstretched hand he held a paintbrush. It had a polished, moon-white handle and bristles so fine they seemed to be spun from silk.

6

Explain that the author has thought carefully about the words she has chosen. She wants the reader to like Ma Liang and feel empathy for him.

Draw the following grid on the board. Initially, just write the names in the grid.

Ma Liang	Old man
• Resourceful • Dedicated • Not greedy	• Is he a good character? • What will he give Ma Liang?

Explain that you are going to think about the characters in more detail.

Read the first paragraph together. Tell the children to talk in pairs about what views they have of Ma Liang from this paragraph. Fill in the grid.

Read the rest of the page together.

Ask the children to share any questions they have after reading this page. (What will the old man give him? Is he a good character? What does this dream mean?)

◀ Turn back to **Respond and return** on page 6

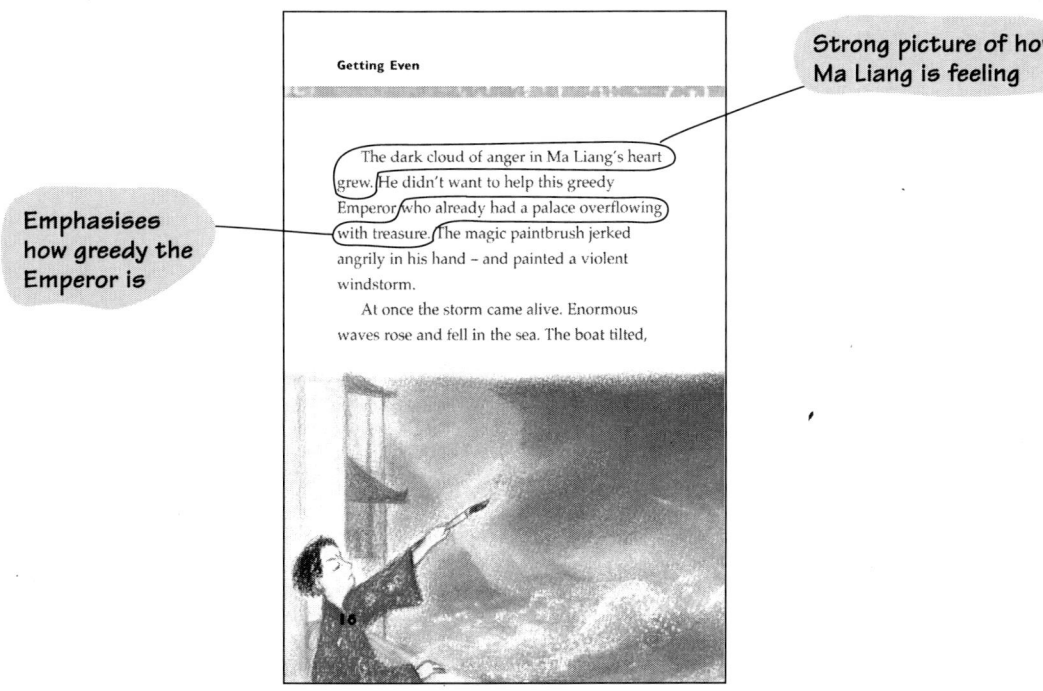

Strong picture of how Ma Liang is feeling

Emphasises how greedy the Emperor is

Getting Even

The dark cloud of anger in Ma Liang's heart grew. He didn't want to help this greedy Emperor who already had a palace overflowing with treasure. The magic paintbrush jerked angrily in his hand – and painted a violent windstorm.

At once the storm came alive. Enormous waves rose and fell in the sea. The boat tilted,

Remind the children that the author has used imagery in this story. This imagery creates a strong picture in our heads, so that we can understand the character's thoughts or feelings better.

Remind the children of the imagery which they have already encountered (his head spun; ate until they almost burst; fever of excitement).

Record the first example of imagery on page 15 on the board: 'The dark cloud of anger in Ma Liang's heart grew'.

Tell the children to draw the picture that the imagery creates in their heads. Share their pictures.

Ask the children to explain what the imagery means. Discuss why the author used this imagery:
- How does it help us understand the thoughts and feelings of the character?

Repeat with the second example 'overflowing with treasure'.

◀ Turn back to **Respond and return** on page 7

Name: _____   **Date:** _____

Part 1

Read page 9 of the text again.

Write in each thought bubble to show what Ma Liang is thinking.

> Ma Liang stared at it and ran his fingers down the gleaming handle. Then he leapt from his mat, mixed a handful of mud with water, dipped the brush in and painted a picture of a horse onto the bare wall of the shack.
>
> As soon as it was finished, there was a loud "*Neigh!*". The next moment, the horse tossed its head – and stepped out from the wall!
>
> It had come alive!

Part 2

What questions do you have:
- about the story?
- about what might happen next?

Write them in the box.

Was it really magic?

READING

PCM
1

Getting Even: The Magic Paintbrush
Skill: Investigating narrative viewpoint

Name: _____ **Date:** _____

Write the opening for a new tale. Use ideas from 'The Magic Paintbrush'.

- The good character is poor. She wants to become a cook.
- She has a dream about being given a magic pot.
- The character is given a challenge. She must only use the magic pot to cook food for poor people.

Long ago there lived a _____ , called _____ had a secret ambition. She longed to be a cook. She couldn't afford to buy any pots or knives but that didn't stop her.

She _____

_____

_____

_____

_____

One night _____ had a strange dream.

_____

_____

_____

_____

_____

_____

_____

Theseus and the Minotaur

Genre: Greek myth
Suggested Renewed Framework
Unit: Traditional stories, fables, myths and legends
Author: retold by William Bedford
Illustrator: David Williams

Key Teaching Objectives

Session 1 / 2
Y5 Strand 6: 1 Spell words containing unstressed vowels
Y5 Strand 7: 2 Infer writers' perspectives

Session 3 / 4
Y5 Strand 7: 1 Use evidence from a text to explain ideas
Y5 Strand 7: 5 Explore how writers produce comic / dramatic effects
Writing
Y5 Strand 9: 2 Write own story; experiment with different styles

At a Glance

Session 1 / 2: Focus on Narrative Viewpoint
Session 3 / 4: Focus on Imagery

This well-known Greek myth is retold in traditional form. It includes all the key features of myths, including being set in a non-specific time, monsters, gods and heroes, curses and challenges, triumph and tragedy.

Imagery is used to describe the emotions of the characters. The violent encounter between the Minotaur and Theseus creates suspense and strong visual images. The conclusion of the story combines victory and tragedy.

Text introduction: activating prior knowledge
Pages 22–24

Remind the children of key features of myths: *ancient traditional story; set in a non-specific time; hero faces challenge; may include: gods, monsters and heroes, curses, triumph and tragedy.*
Explain that this is a myth in which a curse is put on the people of Athens. Explain: the meaning of 'curse'; that Athens is the capital of Greece; that people from there are called Athenians.
Read pages 23 and 24 to the children. Ask them why King Minos wanted revenge. *His son's death.* Identify the sentence that describes the Minotaur. What is it like? *Terrible; it has sharp teeth and huge jaws*

Teaching strategies: phonic/semantic strategies

Recap the reading strategies that help us to read unknown words. Decode the word 'labyrinth' together, reminding the children to use phonic strategies: chunk the word into syllables, sound and blend the phonemes in each syllable and blend the syllables to read the word (l-a-b/y/r-i-n-th). Ask the children if they know the meaning of this word. Remind them about reading on to get extra information. Does the first sentence of the second paragraph on page 24 help us work out what 'labyrinth' means? *No.* Can they predict what it means from the next sentence? *Yes; it tells us it is a maze of twisting, turning tunnels*

Read and discuss: interpretive strategies
Pages 25–29

Introduce the words: 'all-devouring', 'destined', 'curse'. Ask the children to read to the end of page 26 and to find out what the curse is and how it can be lifted. Discuss the story as a group:
• How can the curse be lifted? *Someone must kill the Minotaur*
• Why does King Aegeus weep? *The Minotaur is too strong; the girls and boys are going to certain death*
Now tell the children to read to the end of page 29. Check that they have understood the plot:
• What does Aegeus ask Theseus to do if he succeeds in killing the Minotaur? *Sail home with a white sail*
• Who helps Theseus, and why? *Ariadne; she falls in love with him*
• Do the soldiers think Theseus will be able to kill the Minotaur? How do you know? *No; one of them laughs as he says "find your way out of there"*

▶ Focus on: Narrative Viewpoint • Pages 25–26

Respond and return: questioning
Pages 22–29

Explain to the children that while they are reading, they should be thinking of questions about what might happen next, e.g. 'What is Ariadne's plan?' Invite them to share the questions they have in their heads about what might happen next. Discuss possible answers to their questions.

Follow-up
PCM 3 Investigating narrative viewpoint

Text introduction: prediction
Pages 22–31

Recap the features of myths. Ask someone to summarise what has happened so far. Does this story seem like a myth? *Yes – there is a curse; Theseus is given a challenge; there is a monster*

Invite the children to predict what might happen next in the story, drawing on their knowledge of myths, e.g. Theseus will probably defeat the Minotaur as he is the hero of the story.

Tell the children to read pages 30–31 in pairs. Identify the words and phrases on page 31 that make the Minotaur sound scary.

Myths often include a hero who is given a challenge. Look at the last paragraph. Ask the children which words tell us that it is going to be very difficult to kill the Minotaur. *'His only weapon was a short dagger'; 'His only advantage was surprise'*

Teaching strategies: grammatical strategies

Remind the children of the function of pronouns (pronouns replace a noun and help writing flow by making it less repetitive). Explain that when we are reading we need to check that we understand to whom the pronoun is referring.

Read page 31 together. Identify all the pronouns. Identify who or what each pronoun is referring to. Discuss how we know.

Read and discuss: interpretive strategies
Pages 32–36

Explain that the next section of the story describes the fight between Theseus and the Minotaur. Ask the children to read page 32. Discuss this page as a group:

- How does he kill the Minotaur? *Sneaks up on it while it is sleeping and stabs it in the heart*
- 'I wonder what Theseus will do now.' *Run out of the maze using the magic string to guide him*

Tell the children to read the rest of the story to find out how the story ends. Check that they have understood the plot:

- How do Theseus and Ariadne feel about each other? Where does it tell you? *Page 34 shows us their love for each other*
- Do they get married? Why not? *No; the god Dionysus falls in love with Ariadne*
- 'I wonder why Theseus doesn't change the sail to white.' *He is thinking only of Ariadne*
- Why does King Aegeus kill himself? *He thinks his son is dead*

 Focus on: Imagery • Pages 31–32

Respond and return: questioning
Pages 34–36

Discuss the ending of the story:
- Did you find any part of the ending surprising?
- What did you think was going to happen?
- Would you prefer that the story had a different ending?

Follow-up

PCM 4 Using pronouns appropriately

Synopsis

The angry King Minos puts a curse on Athens as revenge for the violent death of his son. He has a labyrinth built and places a terrifying Minotaur at the centre. Every year he orders fourteen young Athenians to enter the labyrinth to try to kill the Minotaur in order to lift the curse.

One year, Theseus, son of King Aegeus, asks to take the place of one of the youths. Aegeus tells his son to hoist a white sail on his return if he is successful.

Minos's daughter, Ariadne, falls in love with Theseus and secretly helps him. Theseus kills the Minotaur and escapes with the other Athenians and Ariadne. They plan to marry, but one of the gods claims Ariadne as his own bride. Theseus is so broken-hearted that he forgets to indicate to his father that he is alive. Aegeus sees the black sail, thinks his son is dead and kills himself.

Success criteria

- I can recognise and explain the narrative viewpoint.
- I can discuss the author's use of imagery to compare things.
- I can use the text as a model to write an alternative ending.

Assessment focus

AF5 Explain and comment on writers' use of language, including grammatical and literary features at word and sentence level.

AF6 Identify and comment on writers' purposes and viewpoints and the overall effect of the text on the reader.

Further writing

Ask the children to write a happy ending to the myth.

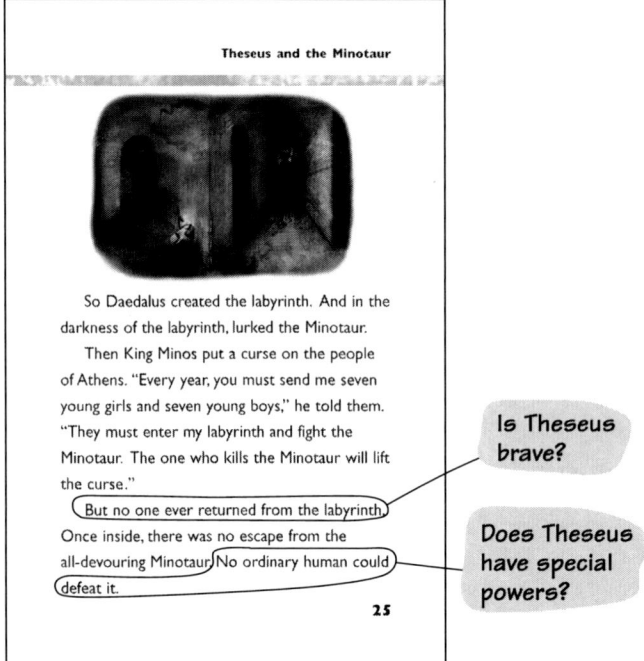

Theseus and the Minotaur

So Daedalus created the labyrinth. And in the darkness of the labyrinth, lurked the Minotaur.

Then King Minos put a curse on the people of Athens. "Every year, you must send me seven young girls and seven young boys," he told them. "They must enter my labyrinth and fight the Minotaur. The one who kills the Minotaur will lift the curse."

But no one ever returned from the labyrinth. Once inside, there was no escape from the all-devouring Minotaur. No ordinary human could defeat it.

25

Is Theseus brave?

Does Theseus have special powers?

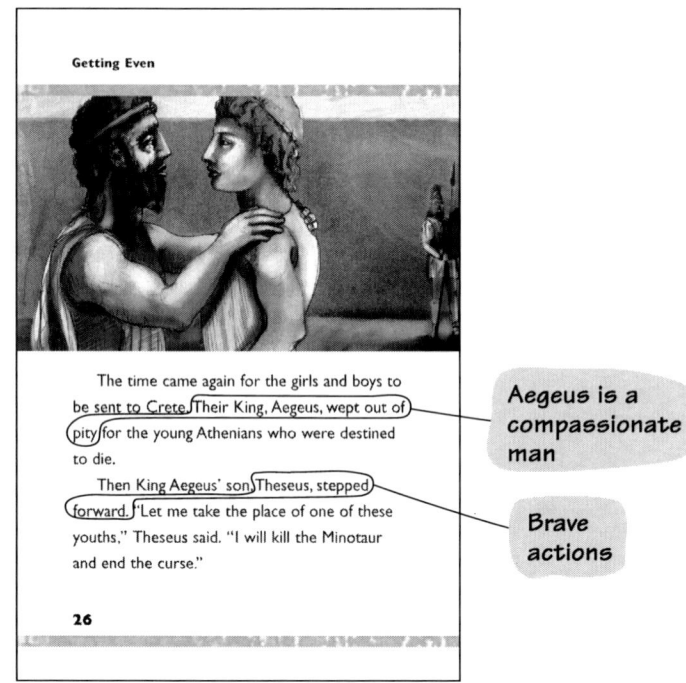

Getting Even

The time came again for the girls and boys to be sent to Crete. Their King, Aegeus, wept out of pity for the young Athenians who were destined to die.

Then King Aegeus' son, Theseus, stepped forward. "Let me take the place of one of these youths," Theseus said. "I will kill the Minotaur and end the curse."

26

Aegeus is a compassionate man

Brave actions

Explain that the author has thought carefully about the words the narrator uses to describe people and what they do. These words can make the reader see the characters in a particular way. He also wants you to see pictures in your head of what is happening.
- Is Theseus brave? What words and phrases tell you this?

Read the first paragraph on page 25 together.
- What pictures do you have in your head?
- How does this make you feel about the Minotaur?

Tell the children to read the final paragraph on page 25 and to decide what this tells us about the character of Theseus.
- What kind of person could defeat the Minotaur? 'I wonder if Theseus has special powers.'

Ask the children to read the first paragraph on page 26 in pairs and to decide how the author wants us to feel about King Aegeus.
- Why does King Aegeus cry? *Because it is an impossible challenge and the young people will die*

How does the author want us to feel about the curse that has been put on Athens? What makes you say that? *Wants us to feel sorry and scared for the young boys and girls; we can see how Aegeus is feeling; labyrinth sounds scary*

◀ Turn back to **Respond and return** on page 12

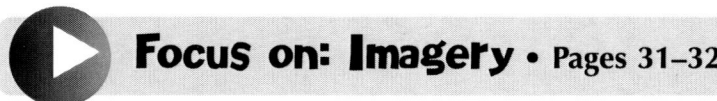

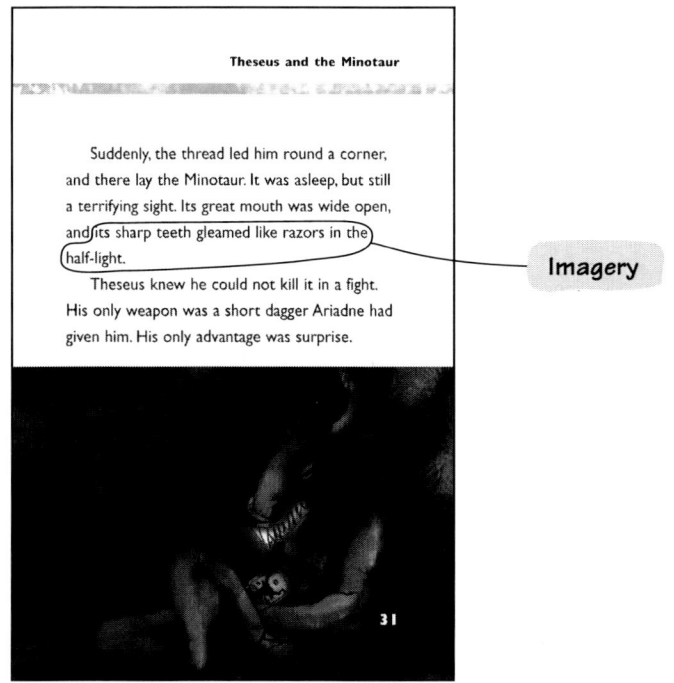

Theseus and the Minotaur

Suddenly, the thread led him round a corner, and there lay the Minotaur. It was asleep, but still a terrifying sight. Its great mouth was wide open, and its sharp teeth gleamed like razors in the half-light.

Theseus knew he could not kill it in a fight. His only weapon was a short dagger Ariadne had given him. His only advantage was surprise.

Imagery

31

Getting Even

Theseus crept close to the Minotaur. Silently, he prayed to the gods. Then he took a deep breath, and yelled the Athenian war cry, "AAEEEIIIAHHHH!"

The Minotaur's eyes flew open in alarm. It struggled to its feet.

Theseus aimed the hilt of his dagger straight at the Minotaur's heart. He hit the Minotaur with all the strength he could find. The Minotaur sank backwards, stunned by the blow.

Turning the dagger round, Theseus aimed the blade straight at the creature's heart, and struck again.

Imagery

"AAEEEIIIAHHHH!" he screamed. The sound echoed like a hundred warcries.

With a horrible choking gurgle, the Minotaur slumped forward. It was dead.

32

Explain that the author has used some imagery in this fight scene to create strong images/pictures of the characters and what is happening.

Remind the children that they have already encountered a form of imagery in 'The Magic Paintbrush' (Ma Liang with the black cloud in his heart; Ma Liang's head spinning with questions).

Explain that in this story, the author uses imagery in a different way. He creates pictures that help us to compare one thing with something else.

Record the first example of imagery on the board: 'like razors in the half-light'. Ask if there were really razors in the half-light? *No*
Explain to the children that there are three useful questions to ask themselves about images, and model answering these questions:
• What is being compared to a razor? *The Minotaur's teeth*
• What do we know about razors? *They are sharp. You use them to cut things. They are made of metal so they would shine in the light*
• How do they make the reader feel? *Cautious; they can be dangerous*

Now ask the children to imagine what the Minotaur's teeth look like. *Sharp and shiny and dangerous*

Discuss why the author chose to use this imagery. *He wanted the reader to see how the Minotaur's teeth were a weapon and could harm people*

Record the next image on the board: '"AAEEEIIIAHHHH!" he screamed. The sound echoed like a hundred warcries.'

Work through these three questions together:
• What is being compared with what? *The echo with warcries*
• What do we know about warcries? *They are loud. They are supposed to frighten the enemy. They show that soldiers are brave*
• How does it make the reader feel? *Excited; Theseus sounds as strong and as brave as a hundred soldiers*

Ask the children to think of an image to describe how the Minotaur looked when he first woke up. 'The Minotaur looked like a _____.'

◀ Turn back to **Respond and return** on page 13

Part 1

Read page 29 of the text again.

How does the author want you to feel about Ariadne? _____

_____

How does the author want you to feel towards Theseus? _____

_____

How does the author want you to feel about Ariadne's father? _____

_____

Part 2

Find each phrase in the text. How does it make you feel about the characters? Record your feelings in the thought bubbles.

I have a plan that will help you

> Ariadne is kind – loves Theseus

You must promise to help me escape – my father is a cruel man

> Ariadne is

Theseus listened

> Theseus is

Pushed him inside

> Theseus feels

"Find your way out of there!" laughed one of the soldiers

> Theseus feels

PCM 3

READING

Getting Even: Theseus and the Minotaur
Skill: Investigating narrative viewpoint

Read the text below. There are too many pronouns and it is difficult to follow the action.

Underline all the pronouns.

Change some of the pronouns to nouns so that the text reads more clearly.

Theseus aimed the hilt of his dagger straight at ~~its~~ ^{the Minotaur's} heart.

With all the strength he could find, he hit it with a sound like the squelching thud of a hammer on a melon.

THWUNK!!!

It sank backwards, stunned.

Turning the dagger round, he aimed the blade straight at its heart and struck again.

'AAEEEIIIAHHHH!' he screamed.

With a horrible choking gurgle, it slumped forward.

It was dead.

Getting Even: Theseus and the Minotaur
Skill: Using pronouns appropriately

WRITING

PCM
4

Genre: Traditional story set in Africa
Suggested Renewed Framework Unit: Traditional stories, fables, myths and legends
Author: Jane Langford
Illustrator: Guy Redhead

Key Teaching Objectives

Session 1 / 2
Y5 Strand 7: 3 Compare structure of different types of text
Y5 Strand 8: 2 Compare usefulness of visualisation / prediction / empathy in exploring texts

Session 3 / 4
Y5 Strand 7: 1 Use evidence from a text to explain ideas
Y5 Strand 7: 2 Infer writers' perspectives
Writing
Y5 Strand 9: 2 Write own story; experiment with different styles

At a Glance

Session 1 / 2: Focus on Features of Traditional Stories and Graphic Novels
Session 3 / 4: Focus on Treatment of Different Characters

This graphic novel tells a traditional story set in Africa. The story deals with some important issues facing many rural areas in Africa: drought, poverty and starvation. The graphic novel style brings the story to life. Children may be familiar with this kind of text or they may need help to recognise such features as narration in text boxes and speech bubbles.

The tale explores the theme of 'good against evil', with good prevailing in the end, but without totally destroying evil.

Text introduction: activating prior knowledge

Pages 39–40

Introduce the title of the story and tell the children that the story is presented as a graphic novel. Ask them to explain what form it will take. Remind them of other graphic novels they have read.
Tell them to read page 40 and to discuss in pairs what they know about the story so far: *setting; characters; type of story*. Share the children's ideas. Tell them that this is a traditional story from Africa. Brainstorm the features of a traditional story: *predictable structure – problem to be resolved; hero who is powerless; evil character who is powerful; can be violent; has a theme and/or moral*

Teaching strategies: constructing images/ inference

Explain that an important reading strategy is to think about the story in your head while you are reading. When reading a graphic novel, you need to be an active reader by:
- Looking carefully at the pictures and who is saying what, and checking the order in which the speech bubbles should be read.
- Asking yourself questions about what characters are saying and doing, e.g. 'Why did he do that?'; 'Is he scared?'
- Predicting what might happen next.
Practise these strategies on page 41.

Read and discuss: interpretive strategies

Pages 41–53

Ask the children to read independently to the end of page 46 and to look out for any features of traditional tales. Discuss the story:
- What is the problem in the story? *Kofi's family has no food*
- What kind of character is Kofi? *Brave, unselfish*
- How is Kofi feeling in the jungle? *Exhausted, frightened, puzzled*
- What kind of character do you think the giant will be? Why? *Fierce, cunning; giants normally have these characteristics*
- 'I wonder what will happen next.'
Tell the children to read to the end of page 53. Check that they have understood the plot:
- How does the giant feel when he first sees Kofi? How does he change, and why? *Angry, but then forms a plan*
- Where do you think Kofi's brother is? Why?

▶ **Focus on: Features of Traditional Stories and Graphic Novels • Pages 46–47**

Respond and return: deduction

Pages 40–53

Discuss the language used by the author, saying 'I wonder why the author wrote: "The giant looked at Kofi, craftily" (page 47) and "He had a cunning look on his face" (page 49).' Ask the children to search for other examples of words or phrases that tell us that the giant may not be trustworthy.

Follow-up
PCM 5 Active reading strategies

Text introduction: monitoring understanding
Pages 40–53

Invite a member of the group to recap what has happened in this traditional story so far. Ask the children who is telling the story. *A narrator – even though much of the story is told via dialogue*

- How do we know which are the narrator's words? *They are in the rectangular boxes*
- Which characters have we got to know? *The giant and Kofi*
- What do we know about them?

Teaching strategies: semantic strategies

Remind the children that if they don't know what a word means, they can:

- Predict by reading the whole sentence
- Look to see if they know part of the word or a similar word
- Use a dictionary

Write three words from pages 58 and 59, e.g. capture, revenge, tangled, or bellow. Ask each pair to take one word, find it in the text and decide what it means. Share the children's definitions and check them in a dictionary.

Read and discuss: interpretive strategies
Pages 54–64

Tell the children to read independently to the end of page 57. What more do they learn about the giant's character? Discuss the story:

- What happens when Kofi gets home? *His brother is missing*
- What clue is there on page 56 that the giant may be an evil character? *Giant has lied to Kofi*
- What is the climax of the story? *Kofi learns that the giant has killed his siblings*
- 'I wonder what will happen next.' (Remind the children about the usual structure of traditional stories and the theme of 'good versus evil'.)

Ask the children to read the rest of the story to find out how the story ends. Check that they have understood the plot:

- How do Kofi's brother and sister come back to life? *Elixir of life spills on their bones*
- How does the giant's eye grow back? *Elixir gets on his ashes*
- Why does Kofi say "the eye can't hurt us"? Is he right? *Because it is just an eye and not the whole giant; no – every time the giant's eye blinks, someone in the world dies*

▶ **Focus on: Focus on Treatment of Different Characters • Pages 56–57**

Respond and return: questioning
Pages 40–64

Hot seating: Invite one child to be the giant. Encourage the others to ask him questions about his actions and behaviour. Repeat with Kofi in the 'hot seat'.

Follow-up

PCM 6 Writing in the style of a graphic novel

Synopsis

Because of drought, Kofi's family is running out of food and water. Kofi leaves home and goes into the jungle to look for food. There he discovers a giant who gives him food in exchange for work. Kofi is happy to stay, until he starts worrying about his family. The giant lets Kofi go back to his family twice on condition that he sends one of his siblings to work in his place. On his return to the jungle, Kofi finds that the giant has eaten his brother and sister.

The villagers kill the giant and discover a potion that brings the two children back to life. It also spills on the giant's ashes, but only his eye grows back. This eye is very powerful, however, and kills someone in the world every time it blinks.

Success criteria

- I can imagine, predict and question when reading.
- I can identify and discuss the features of traditional stories and graphic novels.
- I can recognise and explain the narrative viewpoint.

Assessment focus

AF6 Identify and comment on writers' purposes and viewpoints and the overall effect of the text on the reader.

AF7 Relate texts to their social, cultural and historical contexts and literary traditions.

Further writing

Ask the children to write the brother's or sister's story, in words only.

- What was it like in the jungle?
- What happened when you first arrived?
- What was the giant's house like?
- What happened next?

19

Graphic novels

Ask the children to search for three distinct features of graphic novels.

- Do they enjoy reading graphic novels? Why?
- How is it different from reading a story written without pictures?

Traditional stories

- Who do you meet on these pages and what kind of character do you think he is?
- How do you think Kofi is feeling? Why?

Ask the children to remember the features of traditional stories. List these on the board in a grid (see below).

Give each pair one feature and ask them to find an example in the text.

Fill in the grid, recording examples. The children may decide they don't yet have enough evidence.

Features of traditional stories	Example in this story?
Predictable structure	Opening with problem; build-up with clues that things may go wrong – where is his brother? Is the giant a good character?
Weak but heroic character	Went into jungle alone; went into giant's house
Strong but bad character	Giant thinks the boy may be useful
Can be violent	None yet but haven't reached climax or resolution. However, the giant does roar at Kofi
Traditional theme	Giant may be evil – he looked craftily; cunning look Kofi is good – he wants to save his family

◀ Turn back to **Respond and return** on page 18

Remind the children that this story is told by a narrator whose words are in the rectangular boxes.

Ask them to find an example of a sentence written in the 1st and one written in the 3rd person.
- Whose words are in the 3rd person? *The narrator's*
- In what person are the characters' words written? *1st and 3rd*

Explain that when authors write stories they have a clear picture of the characters and they try to influence how we feel about them.

Ask the children to remember the contrasting characters that often appear in traditional stories. *Good and evil (good character is often brave), weak and strong*

Discuss what we discover on this page. *We find out that the giant is the evil character*

Draw a grid on the board and tell the children to search for examples of things that Kofi does and says which tell you he is a good and brave character. Record these on the grid.

Repeat the exercise, focusing on the giant.

Ask the children to think back in the story – did we know that Kofi was the good character and the giant the evil character? Where are the clues?

 Turn back to **Respond and return** on page 19

21

Active readers:
- Keep the story in their heads like a film
- Predict what might happen next
- Ask questions about the text while they are reading

Draw a film strip recording the main events that have happened in the text so far.

Record your predictions about what you think will happen next.

Record any questions you have about the text so far.

Name: _____   **Date:** _____

What do you think happened while Kofi's brother was at the giant's house?

- Does the giant make him work?
- Is he kind or mean to him?
- Why does he kill him?

Draw the pictures and write the text.

Kofi's brother finally found the giant's house and knocked on the _____

Navigator Max

Written by: Louise Dempsey

                 Denise Margetts

Teaching Guides advisors: Shirley Bickler

                               Michael Lockwood

Rigby

Halley Court, Jordan Hill, Oxford, OX2 8EJ

Rigby is an imprint of Pearson Education Limited, a company incorporated in England and Wales, having its registered office at Edinburgh Gate, Harlow, Essex, CM20 2JE. Registered company number: 872828

www.rigbyed.co.uk

Rigby is a registered trademark of Reed Elsevier, Inc, licensed to Pearson Education Limited

© Pearson Education Limited 2008

First published 2002

This edition first published 2008

ARP Impression 98

British Library Cataloguing in Publication Data is available from the British Library on request.

ISBN 978 0 433 07877 7

Typeset by Red Giraffe
Illustrated by Andrew Pavitt (cover); Lisa Smith (page 5); Liz Pyle (pages 8 and 9); David Williams (pages 14–15); Guy Redhead (pages 20–21 and 23)
Logo artwork by Max Ellis
Printed in Great Britain by Clays Ltd, St Ives plc

Every effort has been made to contact copyright holders of material reproduced in this book. Any omissions will be rectified in subsequent printings if notice is given to the publishers.